NO LONGER PROPERTY OF
ANYTHINK LIBRARIES /
RANGEVIEW LIBRARY DISTRICT

AF148684

Lerner **SPORTS**

JESSE OWENS

TRACK-AND-FIELD LEGEND

TRACY SUE WALKER

LERNER PUBLICATIONS ◆ MINNEAPOLIS

SPORTS THRILLS
MEET
RESEARCH SKILLS

Lerner SPORTS

Free Database Trial: lernersports.com

Copyright © 2023 by Lerner Publishing Group, Inc.

All rights reserved. International copyright secured. No part of this book may be reproduced, stored in a retrieval system, or transmitted in any form or by any means— electronic, mechanical, photocopying, recording, or otherwise—without the prior written permission of Lerner Publishing Group, Inc., except for the inclusion of brief quotations in an acknowledged review.

Lerner Publications Company
An imprint of Lerner Publishing Group, Inc.
241 First Avenue North
Minneapolis, MN 55401 USA

For reading levels and more information, look up this title at www.lernerbooks.com.

Main body text set in Myriad Pro Semibold. Typeface provided by Adobe.

Library of Congress Cataloging-in-Publication Data

Names: Walker, Tracy Sue, author.
Title: Jesse Owens : running for gold / Tracy Sue Walker.
Description: Minneapolis : Lerner Publications, 2023. | Series: Epic sports bios. Lerner sports | Includes bibliographical references and index. | Audience: Ages 7–11 | Audience: Grades 4–6 | Summary: "Jesse Owens has been called one of the greatest athletes in track and field history. Follow his life from running on Alabama roads with his father to winning gold in the 1936 Olympic Games"— Provided by publisher.
Identifiers: LCCN 2022014224 (print) | LCCN 2022014225 (ebook) | ISBN 9781728476520 (library binding) | ISBN 9781728478562 (paperback) | ISBN 9781728482545 (ebook)
Subjects: LCSH: Owens, Jesse, 1913–1980—Juvenile literature. | Track and field athletes— United States—Biography—Juvenile literature. | African American track and field athletes—Biography—Juvenile literature. | African Americans—Biography—Juvenile literature. | Olympic athletes—United States—Biography—Juvenile literature.
Classification: LCC GV697.O9 W35 2023 (print) | LCC GV697.O9 (ebook) | DDC 796.092 [B]— dc23/eng/20220329

LC record available at https://lccn.loc.gov/2022014224
LC ebook record available at https://lccn.loc.gov/2022014225

Manufactured in the United States of America
1-52233-50673-7/29/2022

TABLE OF CONTENTS

WORLD'S FASTEST HUMAN

The year: 1933. The event: the National Interscholastic Championship meet at Stagg Field in Chicago, Illinois. All eyes were on Jesse Owens. People said this track star and recent high school graduate from Cleveland, Ohio, was the best young athlete in the United States.

Owens was already a great athlete in 1933, but he didn't become world famous until he competed at Stagg Field.

FACTS AT A GLANCE

Date of birth: September 12, 1913

League: USA Track and Field; Olympic Games

Professional highlights: won four Olympic gold medals in 1936; set multiple national and world records in track and field throughout his career; named to the board of directors of the US Olympic Committee in 1973

Personal highlights: served as a goodwill ambassador for the US State Department; had three daughters, Gloria, Marlene, and Beverly; started the Jesse Owens Foundation, which provides support to young people

Jesse did not disappoint the crowd. He sprinted toward the broad jump, pushed off with all his might, and soared 24 feet 9.25 inches (7.55 m). Jesse's jump set a new high school record. He jumped with grace and power.

Next, he ran the 100-yard dash. He tied the world record of 9.4 seconds. His final event was the 220-yard dash. The crowd and judges were amazed when he set a new high school record of 20.7 seconds. Jesse Owens received the meet trophy that day. And he was just warming up.

Owens began as a sprinter, but he set many records in the broad jump.

BORN TO RUN

Jesse Owens was born in Oakville, Alabama, on September 12, 1913. His parents were Henry Cleveland Owens and Mary Emma Fitzgerald. His father was a sharecropper. His family paid rent for their home by giving half of the crops they grew to the landowner. His family often struggled to put food on the table.

The Jesse Owens Memorial Park in Oakville, Alabama, includes this statue of Owens running through the Olympic rings.

Owens loved running and pushed himself to run faster than everyone around him.

Jesse Owens was the 10th child born in his family. He ran on the dirt paths through the wooded hills of Alabama. He was skinny and often hungry, but his father taught him leg exercises that helped him develop strong muscles. Jesse's father raced against men from nearby farms and always won. Jesse later said, "I always loved running. . . . You could go in any direction . . . seeking out new sights just on the strength of your feet and the courage of your lungs."

Owens's family moved to Cleveland, Ohio, in the early 1920s. Many Black people living in the South migrated north to create better lives by finding work in mills and factories.

FROM J. C. TO JESSE

Jesse Owens's parents named him James Cleveland and called him J. C. On his first day of school at Bolton Elementary School, Owens murmured "J. C." when his teacher asked his name. She thought he said Jesse instead of J. C. From that day on, he went by Jesse.

Runners line up behind the starting line at a track-and-field event.

When the weather was good, Jesse's class walked to the nearby high school track. Jesse always won short sprints and broad-jumping contests. Charles Riley, the Fairmount Junior High School track coach, watched. He was looking for strong runners and saw that Jesse was one. One day Riley offered to coach Jesse in track and field. Riley wanted to turn Jesse into an athlete.

RACING AGAINST HIMSELF

Jesse's training got serious when he started junior high school. He got to school before the first bell in the morning so he could train with Riley. His training began with stretching to make his muscles flexible and help prevent injuries. After school, Jesse had a job to help his family get by.

In 2010, Cleveland, Ohio, named a street Jesse Owens Way in his honor.

Jesse trained for a lot of different events, including short sprints, the high jump, and the broad jump. He was easy to coach, but sometimes he gave up if he fell behind in a race. Riley taught him not to give up. He told Jesse to focus on racing against himself.

Jesse competed in many track-and-field events, including the long jump. In the long jump, athletes get a running start before jumping as far as they can.

Charley Paddock (*left*) and Jackson Scholz (*right*) were both world-famous athletes and Olympic champions. Paddock was one of Jesse's track-and-field heroes.

In 1928, Charley Paddock spoke at Fairmount Junior High. Paddock was then the most famous track star. After hearing him speak, Jesse had a new dream. "I knew I was going to the Olympics someday, impossible as it seemed," Jesse said.

Jesse started school at East Technical High School in the fall of 1930. The track coach was Edgar Weil. Weil asked Charles Riley to continue coaching Jesse because Riley and Jesse worked well together.

In high school, Jesse grew stronger and taller. He had no trouble beating Cleveland's other high school runners. While this excited him, he had his eyes on the 1932 Olympic Games.

EAST TECHNICAL HIGH SCHOOL.

Many famous athletes attended Cleveland's East Technical High School, including Harrison Dillard, the first athlete to win gold in both the 100-meter sprint and 110-meter hurdles.

THE ROAD TO GOLD

Owens's chance to qualify for the US Olympic team came in the spring of 1932. The Midwest tryouts took place at Northwestern University in Illinois. Owens ran well, but he was competing against some of the best runners in the world. He wasn't ready yet. He did not make the team. But his time would come.

Owens (*front right*) runs at the 1936 US Olympic trials after failing to make the team in 1932.

Before a race, track runners get ready in the set position. The set position helps them launch forward quickly.

By the time Jesse's high school career was ending, college track coaches across the country knew who he was. He could pick wherever he wanted to run in college. He felt a strong loyalty to Ohio, so Ohio State University was a natural choice.

Starting college wasn't easy. His family couldn't afford it. At the time, most schools didn't offer athletic scholarships for track and field. Luckily, Owens got a job running an elevator in the state capitol building in Columbus.

NOT AN EQUAL EXPERIENCE

When Owens attended college, Black students could not live in the dorm buildings. Black people were also segregated from white people in certain public spaces. Owens was in charge of the freight elevator instead of the passenger elevator where white people worked.

Owens married Minnie Ruth Solomon on July 5, 1935.

Owens couldn't compete on the varsity track team in his first year. But he was already breaking and setting many records. In spring 1935, Owens finally joined the varsity team. Stadium crowds and newspaper reporters cheered on his record-setting speed. Later that year, Jesse Owens married Minnie Ruth Solomon, who changed her name to Ruth Owens. She was his high school sweetheart and the mother of his daughter, Gloria.

The next year, Americans were not sure if the US should participate in the Olympic Games. Germany was hosting that year, and the National Socialist (Nazi) Party and Adolf Hitler controlled Germany. The Nazi Party was anti-Semitic and made new laws discriminating against Jews. Hitler blamed Jews for Germany's defeat in World War I (1914–1918). Despite these unfair laws, the US Olympic team still participated in the Olympic Games.

German soldiers line up at a 1935 rally in Nuremberg, Germany.

At the 1936 US Olympic trials, Jesse Owens beat his rival in the 100-meter dash, Ralph Metcalfe (*right*).

In 1936, Owens took part in the United States Olympic trials. He breezed through the semifinals. The finals took place in Randall's Island, New York. Owens won the 100- and 200-meter dashes. He also won the broad jump. Just three days after the Olympic trials ended, Owens and the US Olympic team boarded the SS *Manhattan* for the voyage across the Atlantic Ocean.

Owens was surprised to find out that he was already famous in Berlin, Germany. They knew he was the top American runner. Sports reporters, German citizens, and fellow athletes greeted him in the Olympic Village. They wanted to shake his hand, take his picture, and ask for his autograph.

RACISM IN NAZI GERMANY

Hitler and the Nazi Party declared that white Germans were smarter and stronger than other people around the world. Hitler wanted white German athletes to win at the Olympics to prove he was right. But Jesse Owens challenged these beliefs and showed that Black athletes could win the world's biggest sports events.

FASTER, HIGHER, STRONGER

On August 2, 1936, Owens tied the world record of 10.3 seconds in the quarterfinal race for the 100-meter dash. He also won the semifinals. On August 3, six of the world's best runners competed in the finals. Owens ran with everyone else for the first 30 meters. Then he pulled ahead. He was the clear winner. As Owens said, "The 100-yard dash is a fast race . . . here, you've got to get off with the gun."

On August 3, Owens (*pictured*) beat fellow American Ralph Metcalfe and Dutch runner Tinus Osendarp in the 100-meter dash.

Owens stood on the victory stand with his gold medal around his neck. He had achieved his dream, and the United States had a new hero.

Owens went on to win three more gold medals at the 1936 Olympic Games. His biggest competitor in the broad jump was a young German athlete named Luz Long. Long was the kind of athlete Nazi Germany liked. He was tall, white, and blond. But Owens won the event. Long rushed over to congratulate him, and the two athletes walked off the field together as friends.

Owens (*center*) stands on the Olympic podium to accept a gold medal. German athletes and officials in white salute Hitler, but Owens does not make the offensive gesture.

Owens shows off his four Olympic gold medals.

Owens wasn't finished. He went on to win the 200-meter sprint and set a new Olympic record time of 20.7 seconds. He also helped the US team win the 4 x 100-meter relay. The Berlin Olympics ended after two weeks. Owens won four gold medals. He was the hero of the 1936 Olympic Games.

ONE OF THE GREATEST

After the Olympics, Owens earned money through public speaking, doing radio ads, and selling products. He started a company called Jesse Owens Dry Cleaning Company. He and his wife had two more daughters, Marlene and Beverly.

Owens opened a dry cleaning shop in 1938.

Owens was dedicated to sports and the Olympics for the rest of his life. He received invitations to attend the 1956 Olympic Games in Melbourne, Australia; Mexico City, Mexico, in 1968; and Munich, Germany, in 1972. He was also named to the board of directors of the US Olympic Committee in 1973.

Jesse Owens died from lung cancer on March 31, 1980. Track-and-field fans call him one of the greatest athletes of all time. As he said in the final pages of his book *Jesse,* "I have always tried to do what my father vowed to do—the hardest thing. Always keep the faith."

Ed Sullivan (*right*) presented Jesse Owens with the Mercury Championship Performance Award in 1958.

SIGNIFICANT STATS

Ran the 90-yard dash in 8.6 seconds to set the 1934 world record

Ran the 120-yard dash in 11.5 seconds to set the 1934 world record

Set the world record in 1935 for the 220-yard dash in 20.3 seconds

Set the world record in 1935 for a long jump of 26 feet 8.25 inches (8.1 m)

Won Olympic gold medals in 1936 for 100 meters, 200 meters, 4 x 100-meter relay, and long jump

GLOSSARY

anti-Semitic: hostility toward or showing discrimination against Jewish people

discriminating: unjustly treating a person differently because of things such as race, religion, sex, or age

interscholastic: a competition carried on between schools

meet: a track-and-field competition

relay: a race between teams in which each team member covers a certain part of the track

scholarship: money given to a student to help pay for education

segregated: organized to keep members of different races apart, either by dividing facilities into different sections or creating separate facilities for members of certain races

sprint: a short run at top speed

tuition: money paid for instruction, such as college

varsity: the top team at a school

voyage: a long journey by sea, air, or land

SOURCE NOTES

9   William J. Baker, *Jesse Owens: An American Life* (New York: Free Press, 1986), 11.

14 Jesse Owens and Paul Neimark, *Blackthink: My Life as a Black Man and White Man* (New York: Pocket Books, 1971), 45.

23 Owens and Neimark, 138.

27 Jesse Owens and Paul Neimark, *Jesse: A Spiritual Autobiography* (Plainfield, NJ: Logos, 1978), 201.

LEARN MORE

Buckley, James, Jr. *Jesse Owens*. New York: DK, 2020.

Hoena, Blake. *Jesse Owens*. Minneapolis: Graphic Universe, 2020.

Olympics.com
https://olympics.com/en/athletes/jesse-owens

Scheff, Matt. *The Summer Olympics: World's Best Athletic Competition*.
Minneapolis: Lerner Publications, 2021.

Team USA
https://www.teamusa.org/

USATF Youth
https://www.usatf.org/programs/youth

INDEX

PHOTO ACKNOWLEDGMENTS

Image credits: Bettmann/Getty Images, pp. 4, 7, 16, 17, 19; Vaclav Volrab/Shutterstock, pp. 5, 28; Walter Bibikow/Alamy Stock Photo, p. 8; Popperfoto/Getty Images, p. 9; Suzanne Tucker/Shutterstock, p. 11; Ken Redding/Getty Images, p. 12; Faulbaum/ullstein bild/Getty Images, p. 13; AP Photo, p. 14, 21, 26; FAY 2018/Alamy Stock Photo, p. 15; FPG/Hulton Archive/Getty Images, p. 20; Universal History Archive/Universal Images Group/Getty Images, p. 23; Keystone-France/Gamma-Rapho/Getty Images, p. 24; Hulton Archive/Getty Images, p. 25; Steve Oroz/Michael Ochs Archives/Getty Images, p. 27.

Cover images: AP Photo/Joe Caneva; AP Photo.